T0068023

The Seal of the Living God

A Study of Revelation 4-7
FOR YOUTH

By

Aunt Connye

authorHOUSE

AuthorHouse™
1663 Liberty Drive
Bloomington, IN 47403
www.authorhouse.com
Phone: 833-262-8899

© 2012 by Aunt Connye. All rights reserved.

No part of this book may be reproduced, stored in a retrieval system, or transmitted by any means without the written permission of the author.

Published by AuthorHouse   10/08/2020

ISBN: 978-1-4685-4186-1 (sc)
ISBN: 978-1-4685-4185-4 (e)

Library of Congress Control Number: 2012900692

Print information available on the last page.

Any people depicted in stock imagery provided by Thinkstock are models, and such images are being used for illustrative purposes only.
Certain stock imagery © Thinkstock.

This book is printed on acid-free paper.

Because of the dynamic nature of the Internet, any web addresses or links contained in this book may have changed since publication and may no longer be valid. The views expressed in this work are solely those of the author and do not necessarily reflect the views of the publisher, and the publisher hereby disclaims any responsibility for them.

Breakthrough
COMMUNICATIONS
Constance Ridley Smith © 2010

Contents

Introduction

What Is Your Seal?

"By their fruits you shall know them."
Matthew 7:16

Whenever something is created, the maker or creator of the product attaches a special **seal**. The seal has a special meaning to the person who created it. Sometimes other people do not know what each part of the seal means because the seal often contains symbols.

The symbols stand for something that is important to the creator of the product. Sometimes these symbols are easy to figure out, sometimes they are not.

The process for making the **seal** uses certain 'specs' or specifications.

- Certain colour
- Certain size
- Certain methods of producing the **seal**

These 'specs' set the identity of the product apart from other **'wannabee'** (or similar) products.

Here is my special **seal** for the products that God allows me to create; the BreakThrough **seal**.

I stamp the BreakThrough **seal** on everything that I create.

Here is another Seal of approval:

Think about your favourite:

> Snack
> Sneakers
> Handbag
> Car
> Clothing
> School Crest

Each carries a label or **seal** that lets you know that it is authentic, genuine, real, truly the product that you have come to enjoy.

Check Your Understanding:

A **Seal:**

- lets you know who created the product
- lets you know if something passed the creator's test of authenticity
- lets you know if the item is genuine or fake
- sets something apart from the others
- is an identifying mark

A **seal:**
Keeps freshness in;
Locks contamination out

Would you eat a candy bar if the package were already opened?

☐ yes

☐ no

Would you use a band-aid that was not sealed?

☐ yes

☐ no

You are One of God's precious creations.

God wants to give you His **seal**.
How does God **seal** His believers?
The Bible tells us:

"I will write my law in their inward minds and I will seal them in their foreheads."

"I will put my laws into their mind, and write them in their hearts: and I will be to them a God, and they shall be to me a people."

Hebrews 8:10

"And it was commanded them that they should not hurt the grass of the earth, neither any green thing, neither any tree; but only those men which have not the seal of God in their foreheads."

Revelation 9:4

"I will put my law in their inward parts, and write it in their hearts; and will be their God, and they shall be my people."

Jeremiah 31:33

What does God mean by your "mind,"
your "heart,"
your "inward parts,"
your "forehead"?
The words "mind" and "heart" are closely related.
This type of heart is not the "ticker" on the left-hand side of your chest.

The word "heart" means the "mind," but more important, it means the driver to the decisions we make . . . our control center—what governs our actions.

If your mind and desires are "sealed" by God, what behaviours would others see you do?

What behaviours would they never see you do?

So both of these terms—"mind" and "heart" refer to:

-your thoughts
-your belief system
-your ability to have clear thoughts
-your decision-making abilities

Consider This:

Everything that God has, Satan has a counterfeit.

Our Heart & Mind (what God looks at) . . .

Our Outward Appearance (what the world sees)

God will seal his people.

As you might imagine there will be a true seal and there will be a fake or counterfeit seal.

Hopefully by the time you finish this book, you will only accept the true seal, the Seal of the Living God.

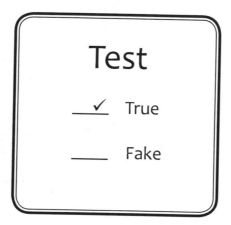

(We will learn more about this as we study Revelation 7).

Before we read chapter 7, let us get an idea of what John saw and experienced in chapters 4, 5, and 6.

New Terms

- **Throne**

- **Emerald**

- **Sardius**

- **Jasper**

- **Elders**

- **Worthy**

Introduction to Revelation
Chapter 4

You may remember the story about the seven churches in Revelation 3. After John received the messages for the 7 churches, God showed him many astonishing things.

In Revelation 4, John saw an open door in heaven, and a voice which resounded like a trumpet said to him, come in here, let me show you what will happen next.

John saw a throne in heaven. It had a rainbow around it, making it look like an emerald (a precious stone which is green in color.) God sat on the throne. The jasper and the sardius stones gave a beautiful burst of colour to His appearance. In front of the throne there was a crystal clear sea—the water was so clear you could see through it. It was like glass.

John heard thunder, lightning, and voices. This was a call for John to pay attention. This was God's signal to John, to let him know that he was about to receive some powerful messages.

There were 24 other thrones placed around God's Throne. Twenty-four elders were dressed in white clothing. They were seated on the 24 thrones around God's Throne. They had golden crowns on their heads.

The story sounds pretty normal so far. Right?

But the next thing that John saw astonished him.

He saw 4 living creatures in the midst of this scene. Each creature had six wings. The creatures were full of eyes; eyes in the front of their heads and eyes in the back of their heads.

The 4 creatures were:

- A lion
- A calf
- A creature having the face of a man
- An eagle

Separately, each type of creature symbolized something special. We will talk about that later, but for now let's focus on the job of these creatures as a group. **Together,** the job of these creatures was to give thanks and honor to God who sat on the throne. Day and night, they moved around and in the middle of the throne crying these words over and over:

"Holy, Holy, Holy, Lord God Almighty, which was and is to come."

Revelation 4: 8

Each time they cried these words, the 24 elders would fall down before God, cast their golden crowns before the throne, and worship Him by saying:

"Thou art worthy, O Lord, to receive glory, and honour, and power: for thou hast created all things, and for thy pleasure they are and were created."

Revelation 4:11

The job of the 4 beasts (creatures) and the 24 elders was to:

☐ Make us all afraid

☐ Show us how created beings should worship their Creator

☐ Give us bad dreams

☐ Worship God

☐ Show us how to worship God

HINT: YOU SHOULD HAVE CHECKED 3 BOXES.

Introduction to Revelation
Chapter 5

In Chapter 5, God was still sitting on the Emerald Throne. In his right hand, he was holding a book that contained writing within it <u>and</u> on the back side.

The book was sealed with 7 **seals**. A strong angel came and asked everyone—"Who is worthy to unfasten the 7 **seals**?"

No one answered.

By now, John was eager to know what was written in the book. He was quite disappointed to learn that he would not find out what was contained in the book. John became sad and cried.

Then one of the 24 elders told John that One Person was worthy to open **seals** so that the book could be read. That One Person was "He who was slain for the sins of the world; none other than the Lamb of God, Jesus Christ."

When the Lamb of God appeared, so did angels.

There were ten thousand times ten thousand, and thousands of thousands of angels, saying with a loud voice,

"Worthy is the Lamb that was slain to receive power, and riches, and wisdom, and strength, and honour, and glory, and blessing."

Revelation 5:12

Then John saw every creature which is in heaven, and on the earth, and under the earth, and in the sea, saying,

"Blessing, and honour, and glory, and power, be unto him that sitteth upon the throne, and unto the Lamb for ever and ever.
And the four beasts said, 'Amen.' And the four and twenty elders fell down and worshipped him that liveth for ever and ever."

Revelation 5: 13-14

Summary of Chapter 5

When Christ took the book in His hand, this symbolized His worthiness to do what no one else was able to do. That is because Jesus Christ did for us what no one else has done. He died on the cross to keep us from having to die for our sins.

Neither the four creatures nor the 24 elders were able to open the **seals**. They were not worthy to do the job.

Because they recognized Christ as being the only One who could do this special task, the four living creatures and the 24 elders fell down before the feet of Jesus Christ. Each one of the elders had a harp and a golden bowl full of incense. The incense represented the prayers of the God's people. With their harps, they sang a new song, saying,

"You are worthy to open its seals, for you, Christ, have given your life to redeem mankind and save them from the penalty of sin."

Revelation 5:9

Introduction to Revelation
Chapter 6

The **seals** were not opened all at once. As the seals were opened, John viewed what was inside the book. He remembered that the 7 churches were symbols of things to come, or events that would take place. He began to realize that the 7 **seals** also symbolized things to come. This is what we mean by "prophecy."

Bible scholars and those who study Bible prophecy believe that five of the **seals** have been opened and the sixth **seal** has been partially opened.

However, the seventh **seal** has not been opened yet.

As the **seals** were being opened, the messages of future events were being unfolded to John. He realized that the six seals were another way that Jesus was revealing what would happen on earth. John realized that the **seals** contained _some of the same messages_ that he had learned when the seven churches were being revealed to him in Revelation Chapter 3. As the seals were being opened, John could not believe his eyes.

Here is what John saw as the Seven Seals were being opened.

	What was Said to John	What John Saw	What Else Did He See?
1st Seal	Come & See	White Horse; (Rev 6:2)	A conquereor; The rider had a bow and arrow and wore a crown,he went to conquer the gospel and overpower it.
2nd Seal	Come & See	Red Horse; (Rev. 6:4)	The rider was given power to kill other people; He had a great sword.
3rd Seal	Come & See	Black Horse (Rev 6:5)	The rider had a balance (scale) in his hand. He weighed out wheat and barley, as if it were a time of famine.
4th Seal	Come & See	Pale Horse (Rev 6:8)	Rider was called Death and hell followed him; he had the power to kill a fourth part of the earth; he killed with death, hunger, and a sword and with the beasts of the earth. (This symbolized people who were killed for worshipping and exercising their beliefs. They are called "martyrs.")
5th Seal		The souls of the Martyrs (Rev 6:9)	The souls of the martyred people cried out, "How long will it be before those who killed the martyrs will be punished?" Each of them was given a white robe and told that they would "rest" until all prophecy and the end time would be fulfilled. They were told that others would also be killed for their beliefs, just as they had been.

6ᵗʰ Seal		White Horse (Rev 6:12-17)	There was a great earthquake; sun became black; moon became as blood; stars of heaven fell to the earth; heaven departed as a scroll; people fled to the mountains and rocks. They were afraid of the wrath of the Lamb of God and pleaded with the "mountains" to fall on them and hide them. They were afraid that they were not ready for the Second Coming of Jesus Christ.
		Special Sealing of God's chosen people (Rev 7:1)	Then John saw four angels standing on the four corners of the earth, holding the winds of strife until all the servants of God were sealed in their foreheads: 144,000 people will get this special seal.
		Another group of people stood before the throne of God and the Lamb of God. (Rev 7:9)	Then a special number-a multitude that no man could number of all nations, kindreds, tongues, stood before the throne. They were wearing white robes. They were crying with a loud voice, "Salvation to our God which sitteth upon the throne and to the Lamb."
7ᵗʰ Seal		7 Angels stood before God. Each was given a trumpet; hence 7 Angels and 7 Trumpets (Rev 8)	There was space in heaven about the space of a half hour.

Introduction to Revelation
Chapter 7

In the space of time between the opening of the sixth **seal** and the seventh **seal**, God will recognize 2 groups of people as His own.

Group 1—The first group of people will receive the Seal of the Living God.

Group 2—The second group will receive white robes and will have palm branches in their hands.

God wants to give His own **seal** to his people, those who serve Him. Perhaps you and I will be in that number.

He wants to **seal** His people to preserve them and keep them through a difficult time that they will face, a time of trouble or tribulation. Without His **seal**, they will not be able to stay on course. With this **seal**, they become "locked in" for the cause of God. No one or nothing will be able to shake the sealed believers from their faith in God, their beliefs, or their destiny to live eternally in Heaven.

This **seal** will be:

— Written in our foreheads
— Identify us as His people
— Will not be seen by others, but it
— Will set us apart, as those who served Him and worshipped Him.

After this group has been sealed, another group containing people of every nation, kindred, and tongue will be recognized. These are they who will have come out of the Great Tribulation (without sinning). They will receive white robes. And God shall wipe all of their tears and fill their hearts with joy. They will never experience any more sorrow, pain, nor death.

There will be silence in heaven for the period of one week as Christ makes the journey with these two groups from earth to Heaven. What a joyous day that will be. This fulfills the miracle of our saviour's birth, life on earth, crucifixion, ascension, and second coming. John saw all of this!

How many believers will the Living God **seal** at this time?

Do the Math:

There were 12 tribes of Israel and 12,000 were counted in each tribe.

How many people of God will be sealed?

Why were they sealed?

God wants to give you His seal.
God's seal is

_____ inward

_____ outward

Guess Who Won't Tattoo?

Today, many people are receiving "outward" seals, that is "on their bodies" where you can see them. The next part of our study will show you why this is not God's plan for you.

If you accept the Bible as a true guidebook for your life, read what the Bible says about placing "seals" on your body.

In both cases, people who practiced such things were either trying to communicate with the dead or trying to please their idol gods.

Here's what the Bible has to say about placing "seals" on your body:

"Ye shall not make any cuttings in your flesh for the dead, nor print any marks upon you: I am the Lord."

Leviticus 19:28

26And they took the bullock which was given them, and they dressed it, and called on the name of Baal from morning even until noon, saying, O Baal, hear us. But there was no voice, nor any that answered. And they leaped upon the altar which was made.

27And it came to pass at noon, that Elijah mocked them, and said, Cry aloud: for he is a god; either he is talking, or he is pursuing, or he is in a journey, or peradventure he sleepeth, and must be awaked.

28And they cried aloud, and cut themselves after their manner with knives and lancets, till the blood gushed out upon them.

I Kings 18:26-28

Fill in the Missing Words

God's way of sealing us is completely opposite from the 'sealing' that is becoming popular today. Many young people are placing **seals** on their bodies. This is not God's plan.

The Bible verses above speak against _____ and _____ one's body.

Cutting oneself is psychologically harmful because it has its roots in Idol _____.

The True and Living God does not require a blood sacrifice from us.

How cool is that?

"The wages of sin is death, but the gift of God (which was made available to us by Jesus Christ's sacrifice at the cross) is eternal life."

Romans 6:23

We make a mistake when we adopt practices that are like those who do not worship the Living God. The Living God does not require any blood sacrifices.

Between the Old Testament and the New Testament, God dealt with the sacrifice-for-sin issue once and for all.

Drawing blood and offering our own sacrifices is not what God requires from any of us. He had one sacrifice—Jesus Christ, the innocent Lamb of God. Christ died once for all mankind.

We should never feel that we need to make such a sacrifice again.

We only need to accept the blood of Christ as the payment for our sins.

It's that easy!

What evidence do we have from the Bible about how God wants us to worship Him, the True and Living God?

Paul reminds us of our spiritual forefathers who trembled and feared God. Their sins separated them from God. They were superstitious and afraid. The first part of the Bible text below shows this—how man viewed God in times of old. Since the cross, man has been reconciled to God through Jesus Christ. The relationship between man and God should still be one of respect, but also one of joy and connection.

 "You have not come to a mountain that can be touched and that is burning with fire; to darkness, gloom and storm; to a trumpet blast or to such a voice speaking words that those who heard it begged that no further word be spoken to them, because they could not bear what was commanded: "If even an animal touches the mountain, it must be stoned to death." The sight was so terrifying that Moses said, "I am trembling with fear."

But you have come to Mount Zion, to the city of the living God, the heavenly Jerusalem. You have come to thousands upon thousands of angels in joyful assembly, to the church of the firstborn, whose names are written in heaven. You have come to God, the Judge of all, to the spirits of the righteous made perfect, to Jesus the mediator of a new covenant, and to the sprinkled blood that speaks a better word than the blood of Abel.
Hebrews 12:18-24

Today's young people are living in a world of mixed messages and confusing signals. It is quite easy for true and fake worship choices to become mixed.

These days, many movies and other media may subtly introduce us to the practices of idol worship. When we are accustomed to seeing these images and practices every day, it becomes easier for us to accept the messages of idolatry.

Once we accept part of it, it becomes easy for other emblems and symbols of these practices to creep into our lives, without our recognition.

Many people have started the seemingly harmless practice of face painting. This can pave the way for receiving permanent tattoos. It's like a dress rehearsal. It makes young people "feel okay" with the idea of marking on their bodies.

Let us pray to keep our minds free and clear from these practices.

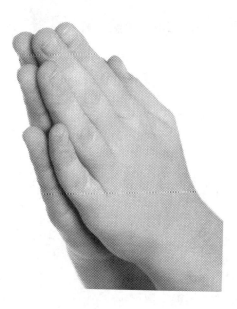

Let's drop in on a conversation two people were having about this very issue:

Q: Why is piercing and tattooing a big issue?
A: Because they both belong to a practice called body modification.

It actually goes back to rites, rituals, and sacrifices that started way back in the Bible days of worshipping idol gods . . . . and body modification is a form of worship.

Q: Wait a minute . . . . I'm not an idol worshipper, at all. I go to church—I'm a Christian.
A: I know you are . . . . but body modification draws blood. Many young people don't realize that when they pierce and tattoo, they are placing themselves on the borderline for adopting the habit-forming practices of idol worship. It can even open the gate which leads to many more piercings and cuttings.
Q: How's that? I only want one little rose on my arm . . . . it will be cute. My grandmother's name was Rose and I want to always remember her. I'm a little scared, but I want that rose on my arm.
A: Well, you're like most people who have gotten tattoos. Most people are a little frightened before they get their first piercing. But sometimes the thrill of the piercing gives them a little rush—even a lightheaded exhilaration.

This can cause them to want to experience that feeling again. Before you know it, they have scheduled another piercing. The human brain records each one of our experiences and codes them as pleasure-giving or pain-giving. Of course in piercing there is a slight pain, but for many people—depending on how their brain records the experience—they will seek more piercings or tattoos to subconsciously receive and relive the feeling of pleasure. And just because of how we are made, it often takes a greater amount of the body piercing or cutting to produce the same feeling of pleasure.

So it's very likely that your mind will not allow you to be satisfied with the one rose. You're likely to be driven by your own mind to get a larger tattoo or multiple tattoos.

In fact, whenever a human being bleeds, there are certain chemicals that are released in the body that soothe and calm the person. When you fall down and scrape your knee, it bleeds, but the body releases the chemicals to begin healing itself and repairing the trauma. It gets complicated, but without knowing what they are doing, or why, people can get hooked on the feeling or the sensation that marking the flesh and piercing creates. If they are hurting inside (emotionally), they may begin to subconsciously schedule another piercing or tattoo to receive the release of chemicals that soothe.

Q: You said that they are placing themselves on the borderline for adopting bad practices of idol worship. That's a bit "out there" in left field isn't it?

A: Not really. Here's why: All gods require a sacrifice. In Bible days, idol worshippers built fires to bring in the presence of the idol god.

Then they knew that worship required a sacrifice. That sacrifice was usually human blood. Sometimes people offered their children to these idol gods.

Sometimes they danced around the fire and cut themselves until their skin would bleed to show the idol god that they honoured him.

Read your Bible: I Kings 18:24-39. I have placed it here in the King James Version, but read it in your favorite version for comparison. This is what God's prophet Elijah said to the prophets of the idol god named Baal:

²⁴And call ye on the name of your gods, and I will call on the name of the LORD: and the God that answereth by fire, let him be God. And all the people answered and said, It is well spoken.

²⁵And Elijah said unto the prophets of Baal, Choose you one bullock for yourselves, and dress it first; for ye are many; and call on the name of your gods, but put no fire under.

²⁶And they took the bullock which was given them, and they dressed it, and called on the name of Baal from morning even until noon, saying, O Baal, hear us. But there was no voice, nor any that answered. And they leaped upon the altar which was made.

²⁷And it came to pass at noon, that Elijah mocked them, and said, Cry aloud: for he is a god; either he is talking, or he is pursuing, or he is in a journey, or peradventure he sleepeth, and must be awaked.

²⁸And they cried aloud, and cut themselves after their manner with knives and lancets, till the blood gushed out upon them.

²⁹And it came to pass, when midday was past, and they prophesied until the time of the offering of the evening sacrifice, that there was neither voice, nor any to answer, nor any that regarded.

³⁰And Elijah said unto all the people, Come near unto me. And all the people came near unto him. And he repaired the altar of the LORD that was broken down.

³¹And Elijah took twelve stones, according to the number of the tribes of the sons of Jacob, unto whom the word of the LORD came, saying, Israel shall be thy name:

³²And with the stones he built an altar in the name of the LORD: and he made a trench about the altar, as great as would contain two measures of seed.

³³And he put the wood in order, and cut the bullock in pieces, and laid him on the wood, and said, Fill four barrels with water, and pour it on the burnt sacrifice, and on the wood.

³⁴And he said, Do it the second time. And they did it the second time. And he said, Do it the third time. And they did it the third time.

³⁵And the water ran round about the altar; and he filled the trench also with water.

³⁶And it came to pass at the time of the offering of the evening sacrifice, that Elijah the prophet came near, and said, LORD God of Abraham, Isaac, and of Israel, let it be known this day that thou art God in Israel, and that I am thy servant, and that I have done all these things at thy word.

³⁷Hear me, O LORD, hear me, that this people may know that thou art the LORD God, and that thou hast turned their heart back again.

[38]Then the fire of the LORD fell, and consumed the burnt sacrifice, and the wood, and the stones, and the dust, and licked up the water that was in the trench.

[39]And when all the people saw it, they fell on their faces: and they said, The LORD, he is the God; the LORD, he is the God.

Q: Hey . . . . but I'm not worshipping an idol . . . . I just want a tattoo because it looks good. It's stylish.

A: That may be true . . . . but in order to understand a thing, you've got to understand the beginning of a thing.

A: Many young people get tattoos and piercings because they think it looks good—it's high fashion—it's sexy.

After all who doesn't want to be fashionable and sexy?

But hang with me and let me bring you up to speed about this fashion craze . . . .

Let me tell you what the Bible says about it and then you make your own choice . . . .

Q: How could this be all wrong?

Well . . . . you're right, the idol worshippers had one thing correct . . . .

A: I don't believe it . . . . you're saying that there is a possibility that piercing and tattoos are alright . . . . Can't wait to hear it!

A: These idol worshippers had something correct, because God also requires a sacrifice—sin does require blood and death. That was the Ceremonial law that God set up.

Q: I can't believe it . . . . even you Christians have to give up blood to the Almighty God?

A: Well WE don't have to bleed for our God . . . . He took care of that for us. Here's how.

In Bible days, there were three types of laws:

Civil—to tell them how to live peacefully with each other

Moral—to tell them how to be in harmony with God

Ceremonial—to tell them how to pay for their sins (make sacrifice for their sins) and restore harmony with God

(The Bible verses you just read in I Kings 18 describes God's ceremonial law and the practice of making sacrifice)

Moral Laws included the Ten Commandments as well as extra laws that God gave to Moses. These are recorded in the book of the Bible called Leviticus.

Leviticus is a word that means "Law."

Here is what is written in the book of Leviticus about body modification:

Ye shall not make any cuttings in your flesh for the dead, nor print any marks upon you: I am the Lord.

Leviticus 19:28

They shall not make baldness upon their head, neither shall they shave off the corner of their beard, nor make any cuttings in their flesh.

Leviticus 21:5

The Prophet Jeremiah spoke about cuttings upon the hands of the Moabites. But this was done as a punishment for their unfaithfulness to God. Here is the curse that Jeremiah spoke to the Moabites:

For every head shall be bald, and every beard clipped: upon all the hands shall be cuttings, and upon the loins sackcloth.

Jeremiah 48:36-38

Q: How do we know that this was a curse?

A: We know it is a curse because sackcloth is the type of garment that was used in time of mourning.

When King Ahab was told that his wife, Jezebel would be killed and her blood would run in the street and be licked by dogs. The Bible says, Ahab

"rent his clothes, and put sackcloth upon his flesh, and fasted, and lay in sackcloth, and went softly."

(1 Kings 21:27)

When Mordecai wished to mourn the plight of the Jews, he "put on sackcloth with ashes, and went out into the midst of the city, and cried with a bitter cry."

Esther 4:1

These are just a few examples, but I'm sure you get the point by now: sackcloth, ashes, unnecessary piercings, cuttings in the flesh, and shavings all go together—and it's not a happy status. It's not what the Almighty God wants for His people.

He has a better plan for us.

The Holy Bible tells us that:

> All have sinned and come short of the glory of God."
>
> Romans 8:28

Sin separates humans from God—because God has no sin in Him—He is God.

In the Bible days God's people brought innocent lambs to the altar to become the sacrifice for their sins—because, remember, sin separates man from God. But they were making a mockery of this system of sacrifice—and killing too many lambs. In other words, they were sort of missing the point. So God began to work the second plan that was decided upon during his Creation of the earth. It was called the Plan of Redemption.

The Marvelous Plan of Redemption

Here's how it works:

1. The wages of sin is death (which includes bleeding), but the gift of our God is eternal life through Jesus Christ, our Lord.

2. By one man's death, we all live.

3. He sent His only begotten Son—Jesus Christ, to die on Calvary. Christ shed His precious blood once and for all so that all who accept Him and believe in Him should not perish, should not have any need to cut themselves, destroy their bodies, or reduce the quality of their life by causing their bodies to bleed.

Tattooing is just a bit too close to the practice of offering sacrifices.

Aren't you glad that there is a God who loved us enough to free us from the need to harm ourselves?

We are sealed by his love!

What Should I do about my tattoo?

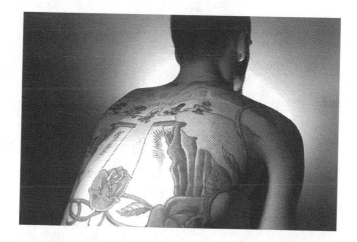

1. Tell God that you accept the One-Time Sacrifice by Jesus Christ as the payment for your sins and shortcomings.
2. Each morning when you awake, ask God for this daily blessing:

   "Lord, show me how to connect with You when I get the urge to pierce, cut, or tattoo my body. God please help me to realize my body is the Temple of the Living God and that I should not mark or graffiti that Temple where you and I alone can dwell."

3. Thank God for showing you His truth about tattoos.
4. Go and tattoo no more.
5. Let others know the truth that you now understand.
6. Ask God to set His seal in your mind and inward parts.

THE END

Be blessed.

Love,
Aunt Connye

References

Text

Review and Herald Publishing Association. 1993. "The Four Horsemen of Revelation, A Bible Prophecy Adventure." Keene, Texas: Review and Herald Publishing Association, pp. 3-4.

The Holy Bible Authorized King James Version. 2001.
Nashville, Tennessee: Thomas Nelson, Inc.

Online
www.biblegateway.com

www.blueletterbible.com

http://healthmad.com/mental-health/10-reasons-people-cut-themselves/#ixzz0q7CNcNna

Discussion of Sackcloth and Ashes at
http://www.cvillechurch.com/Articles/Article_Sackcloth AndAshes.htm

Vine, W. E. "Create, Creation, Creator, Creature", *Vine's Expository Dictionary of New Testament Words*. Blue Letter Bible. 1940. 24 June, 1996 22 Mar 2012.
<http://www.blueletterbible.org/search/dictionary/viewTopic.cfm?type=GetTopic&Topic=Create,+Creation,+Creator,+Creature&DictList=9#Vine's>

Blue Letter Bible. "Dictionary and Word Search for zōon (Strong's 2226)". Blue Letter Bible. 1996-2012. 25 Mar 2012. < http:// www.blueletterbible.org/lang/lexicon/lexicon.cfm?Strongs=G2226&t=KJV >

Vine, W. E. "Beast", Vine's Expository Dictionary of New Testament Words. Blue Letter Bible. 1940. 24 June, 1996 25 Mar 2012. <http://www.blueletterbible.org/search/dictionary/viewTopic.cfm?type=GetTopic&Topic=Beast&DictList=9#Vine's>

Oral
Interviews with people who have gotten tattoos and have practiced cutting

Thank Yous

Copy editing and layout consultation by C.Amber Smith
Jeanann Bassett for data entry.

Sandray Fostin, Silent Nite Creations, Bermuda/Wales
for consultation on Cover Design

Pastor Ulric Hetsberger for providing a content review.

Printed in the United States
By Bookmasters